her

MITALI MEELAN

for the girls with a loud laugh and a soft heart

Foreword

This book is for you—for the moments you feel like you can take on the world and for the days when you just want to be held.

"Her" explores all the beautiful, messy, cozy, loving, angry, and powerful sides of a woman—because let's face it, we are never just one thing—not even in the same month!

I call these poems little murmurs of her heart.

The book is divided into four sections. As you read, I hope the words wrap around you like a comforting blanket in "She Whispers", help you to see the beauty and pain of growing in "She Speaks", empower you to break your silences in "She Screams", and nudge you to embrace the divine feminine within in "She Awakens".

Table of Contents

She Whispers

Her

it's time to let go, darling
the universe is waiting for your hands to be empty
so it can fill it up with everything
you deserve
and *more*.

"what is all this weight I'm carrying in my heart?"

it's the weight of all the hearts
you mended on the way, my love
and forgot to bury the pain you took over.

Her

you will get there
with your feet aching, maybe
and back a little broken
with a few relations catching dust
lying unattended somewhere…
        …maybe a coffee date will revive them?

you will get there
with takeaway dinners
with a bit of messy hair
and dirty nails
and undone laundry
for a few days in a row

but you will get to the place you want to be

soon.

it's okay
your love spilled in places
that didn't deserve it

maybe those were the corners
that needed it the most.

letting go is an art
only those with the strongest of heart
and the softest of love
have ever done it gracefully.

- learn the art my love, it will come in hand

oh darling
the days that you're so afraid to face
is where the courage
you're looking for
is hidden.

Her

dreams come true only
for the most stubborn of hearts.
universe has a way
of pouring blessings on those
who refuse to leave the rain.

meeting the right man
will feel like meeting the
healed
 loved
  grounded
   and *bloomed*
version of yourself.

it might not be okay for now
but it will be okay eventually

your body will find its peace again.
nothing that hurts so much
can live in you forever.

a man who has your back
will melt your insecurities
in the warmth of his arms
and show you just how easy you are to love.

Her

patience
is nothing but knowing what's yours
will always find a way to you.

darling,
some separations
betrayals
heartaches
and crushing changes
will bless your life.

~ allow it to

Her

all her life
she's travelled way too far
trying to find home
in places and people
only to find it when
she stopped her feet and
turned to the mirror.

forming a bond takes time
let it simmer
in conversations and coffees.
let it sit with silences
and learn to enjoy the pauses.
let it greet you with a familiar gaze,
and not a hurried, hungry one
let it learn how to fight
and how to mend.

let it unfold
in its own sweet time

and through it all,
be gentle with your own heart first
before you're gentle with his.

~ unsurety is not a sin

Her

leave it behind, darling
or at least set them down
for a while

the burdens you carry
will only slow you down.

the noise of the world
will shut down
when you start to listen
and honor your own.

I did my part
I mended your heart
that you handed me in pieces.
now that you seek it back
I hope mine finds a mender, too.

keep the ones close
who heard your words
when you never uttered any.

spending time alone, going out for walks with earphones on, making grocery shopping trips, exploring a new restaurant in the city, reading a book, cooking for self, and feeling the life beat within you through it all… are all the whispers of a good life we often forget to hear.

it's not the big achievements
you remember your life by.
it's the little joys you collected
along the way.

~ what little joy did you collect today?

Her

I have a few 'sorry's to say
lying somewhere in my drawer
like unsent letters…

but notorious silence has buried them all.

being yourself will be enough
with the man
who's been sent to love you right.

Her

"will you stay?" she asked, the words barely leaving her lips.

"yes," he replied, "even when you belong to someone else."

~ *a love like that*

rest your feet and
comfort your mind
what your heart so desperately longs for
will find its way into your life.

doesn't her laugh
dance in the air
like your favorite melody?
it reminds you
of the warmth of a
worn out sweater
on the coldest night.

hold on to the ones
who hear your words when you say nothing
see the hurt when you avert your eyes
and hold you tighter when you ask them to go away.

she's been the girl
who cried the nights
and woke up the next day
with a smile.
oh, what power she holds
who's been the storm
and the calm *both*.

some words just feel
like a long, warm hug to her:

"this reminded me of you"
"did you eat?"
"let me cook"
"I'm here"
"what you feel is right"
"take your time"
"you'll get there"
"I love seeing you smile"

eventually
you meet the one who makes you believe
love was simple all along.

"how do I know he's the right one?"

he will speak the language of love so fluently
you will learn to love yourself again.

the right man
will see all your flaws
and fall harder in love with you.

all hearts eventually
find home where peace is,
with a place
or a person.

boredom in a healthy relationship
is a luxury often masked under
security
loyalty
trust
routine
support...

don't mistake it for a lack of spark

- for sparks can only take you so far

a man who truly loves you
will love you when you
least
expect
him
to.

eventually,
you won't have to guess
wait or plead…
the one meant for you
will make love perfectly obvious.

if that's not strength,
then what is?
a heart that shatters
but still knows how to mend and try again
and again and yet *again*.

Her

~ artist

he dipped the tip of his brush in an ocean,
used colors from the palette sky
and painted a picture of a woman
he loved the most.

she was draped in clouds
a bright orange sun over her forehead
her skin a shade of mud brown
her eyes, a constellation at night.

each time he tried to paint
the one he loved the most,
he ended up painting his mother.

She Says

Her

oh, be careful what you say to her.
she's buried more graves
with her words
than her hands.

I saw a leaf fall from a tree.
I asked it, "why let go?"

it replied, "because sometimes,
falling is the only way you learn to fly."

each time you
          choose
          yourself,
you teach the world how to love you.

who's the right one?

a man once asked me, "what's the guarantee that what we feel now will stay the same for the next 30 years?" I had no answer.

then came *he* who pulled me into a sudden hug one lazy afternoon and said, "gosh, we're already 30! I have, what, only 40 more years with you? damn!"

and I stumbled into the answer when I wasn't even looking.

the decision of marriage
should not feel like
a leap in the void but a gentle landing.
not a cage you're getting locked in
but a freedom you're walking into.

- does it feel like that yet?

take up space, darling.
the world belongs to you
as much as it does
to anyone else.

allow yourself
to be surprised by
what you're capable of.

a walking breeze she was
that carried the scent of wilderness
and blooming flowers
both at the same time.

it was a powerful love
that saw all the cracks
and unkempt corners of my soul
and chose not to look away.

your body will know
it has found a home in a man
long before you do.
listen to it, and
trust where it chooses to settle.

darling,
with the right man
love will be patient
trust will be easy
bond will be unforced
comfort will be routine
arguments will be fruitful
and your happiness will be prioritized.

- there won't be room for doubts

a man who stopped at her hesitation
and held her consent above everything else
won her heart.

~ the one who cracked the code

loving yourself becomes so much easier
when you distance yourself from those
who don't love you back.

when life doesn't go as per your plans,
know that what's planned is
far better than anything you can imagine.

comfortable job
cozy home
nourishing food
a few people to love
and a quiet life that doesn't disrupt
by tying a knot to a stranger
or with innocent night-walks home alone,
or with the choice of clothes and degrees.

women want
what men have been granted
since ages.

the simple freedom
to just be.

don't be afraid to fail, darling
the weight of success is heavy,
only failure can make you
strong enough to hold it.

I knew I'd met
the right man
when he greeted me
with fire in his eyes
but wait in his touch.

sometimes, the hardest part is
not finding your way
but believing you *can.*

Her

in his eyes
she was never too much
but always enough
in anger
  in frustration
    in sobs
or accidental snorts that escaped her laughter
in the way she danced and in the way she fell.

in his presence
she felt safe to be silly
and to let her heart sing with
the innocence of a thousand giggles.

her man never said he loved her
but he cherished her inner child
and that's how she knew he did.

just try

so many give up before they even begin.
so write that book
and hit publish
with flutters in your belly
and ink-stained fingers
and doubts crawling on your skin.

join the gym
and stumble in once in a while

confess to that guy
you swore to stay away from
just because you think
he could never love someone like you

say yes more often
and a stern no when it matters
get down and dirty with your dreams
hype yourself
be delusional
be daring.

maybe nothing will work out
but maybe… *it will?*

Her

she searched for the meaning of love
in men who could never teach her well.

and then he came along,
carrying the wisdom of ages
packed in one simple word
that defined love –

acceptance

of everything she was
and everything she couldn't be.

the best thing you can do
for the man you love
is to love yourself first,
and fiercely

take care of that heart,
that body, that soul

fill yourself up with laughter
and wholeness

for no one has ever been able to
pour from an empty cup.

they tell you to be
the heart of the home
but forget that your heart
needs a home, too.

doubts

so many of these little buggers crawling in and out of her mind. one day, she will drag each one by their legs, toss em out, and burn them alive. let their screams give her empty mind some peace. but right now, she'll count them like sheep as she sleeps, even though they are the ones that won't let her.

most days, you need to be
your own hero
so put on your cape, darling,
get off the floor
wipe off the tears
and save your day.

- for no battle is tougher than your fight

what they call weird in you
is in fact your *magic*.

embrace it.

She Screams

Her

in a world that
constantly demands you
to man up

don't forget those
feminine urges
and feminine rage
those resting days
and those conquering ones

remember,
whatever he can
you have done it bleeding.

they all chose the bear
not because of what he was capable of
but because of what he *wasn't.*

remember not to accept compliments
for your silences and servitude.
they are just piling up flowers
on the grave of your voice
so you forget why it bothers you so much.

she's not a rebel
she's just a woman who has
finally realized your world
is not where she wants to live

she wants to *create*
   her
   own.

it wasn't the witches
or the dresses
that made them gather in fear.

it wasn't the wisdom
or the union with nature
women were gifted with,
it wasn't the childbearing power
or the intuition
that made them gather in fear.

it was simply the power of a woman
that refused to be silenced.

I was parched
and your eyes promised an ocean.
so much water,
yet barely a drop to drink.

we are not superhumans,
don't call us that.

it strips away our right
to feel human
to get tired
to break down
to pause
to rest
to revive

as if we should carry it all every day
without a whisper of weariness.

we're not superhuman
just call us a *human*.

darling, you can change
the fate of the women
who follow you
just by being
the woman who
doesn't shrink herself
to fit others in.

Her

inside her head,
there's a storm she's still learning
to weather alone.

stop saying things
to keep the peace
and say things
exactly the way
your mind forms the words
and your lips burn to speak.

she can, you know?
do it right
do it fast
do it well
and perhaps do it better
if the world just stops telling her "you can't."

it's still happening in the cities

there are women
still sitting down
to let the men have the sofas
still eating in the kitchen
to let the men eat at the table
still getting up
when they see one approaching

as if they're less of a life
and less worthy of respect.

promise me
you won't be one of them.
you will hold your head high
and honor your mind
recognize your light
and value your space in the world
despite the packaging you came in with.

Her

whether it's the prison
of money or love
it will wear out
as long as it has bars
and rules.

keep the doors of your home
and your heart
wide, wide open for her
to run away

then every morning you'll find her
greeting you like the sunrise.

the stories of brave women
were left unheard
like whispers in the shadows
and unseen like the soil beneath the feet.

let's make them proud now
for having fought for us
let's do more than what they could
and more than what we think we can

let's finish what they started…

to live,
finally,
on our terms.

what's for dinner?

they burned witches with a mind
and won't let women leave the house.

oh, the world has come a long way.
Now, see!
shoulder-to-shoulder
they work
they roam
they earn
like they've always known how to.
oh,
there's nothing more beautiful
than a free woman.

says my father, with pride
then proceeds to ask my mother
"what's for dinner?"

choose the home
choose servitude
choose the kids
choose to work
in a world that asks women
to choose it all
every day
all day
and all at once

choosing yourself
can be a rebellious act of self-love.

Her

you've been lied to for far too long.

your voice was never too loud or too bossy
your stance never too manly or meek.

your passion was never too forceful
your ambition never too much

your acts of self-love were never selfish
your desire to outsource mundane chores
was never a sign of weakness.

and your desire to want or
not want kids or a husband
was never up for debate.

- we've been lied to for far too long.

slowly,
the women often
lose themselves in all the roles
they are asked to play.

don't be that woman.

make time to play
make time to paint
make time for art
make time for travel
and make time to relax

no one will give you a reward
for the sacrifices

and no one will gift you the time
unless you make it for yourself.

wake up,
you're a Woman

your voice has the power
to rip through the numbing
subjugation like a colossal scream
that shakes the earth.
you have the force of sisterhood
behind you.

wake up,
you're a part of us

you're a Woman.

let the wild ones
amongst us
paint the dark corners
of the world
with their burning ambition
and unrestrained, raucous laughter.
they will bring the change
the future women
will thank us for.

Her

he built a prison and called it home,
caging a bird under the pretence of protection.
but the bird eventually
heard the echoes of freedom
from those outside the window.

now it's only a matter of time
when the *flock* crashes in
to rescue her
and strips all his lies
naked to the bones.

~ *once she learns to fly*

woman was always
a storm they tried to contain
in a tea cup

no wonder they were
eternally intimidated
by what she was capable of.

Her

you'll never be good enough
for the world.
your laugh will be too loud
your jeans too tight
your face will be too dark
your mouth too right
your hands will be too rough
your legs too wide
your passion will be too strong
your manner too wild.

you'll either be too much
or too little
for the world.
why then be anything for it at all?

~ for a change, be good enough for yourself

for a while
let's set down the weight
we were never meant to carry.
the weight of
customs and traditions
marriage and relations
honor and beauty
and the crushing weight of
keeping the world gentle and sane.

Her

they say her role
is to nurture

but who nurtures her
when she is lost
in the giving?

so many superwomen
tuck away their wonder
to herd the families.

I've seen so many superwomen
but never a woman
who removed her cape
and allowed herself to just exist,
without apology,
resting,
and unbothered.

let her be.
let her create more than a child
let her create more than a home
let her voice echo in halls of power
let her be free and disgraceful
let her be loud and driven
let her seek the dawn
let her walk the nights
when she harms no one… let her be.

let her ask the questions
and seek why she was born
with a fiery mind and an ice-cold heart
let her escape the rules, the fears
the noose, the tears
let her live and let her create
not for the world
but for herself.

for *once*,
let her be.

and then I said *no*.

a word rotten in the pit of my throat for decades. it refused to turn into manure, just stuck there like a bone, suffocating generations of women. those who came before me, passed down the bone like the only piece of food they earned on their own. finally, I purged the rot, let it linger on my tongue and it turned into a glowing piece of fire. it stayed there, but only for a moment, for it burned so wild, it set the whole world ablaze.

so I finally spit out my *no*. it only turned into manure when it left my mouth, the manure that bloomed a garden for generations of women who followed.

Her

"Where is all the rage coming from?"

from the shallow ends
of the prison cell
crowded by women
with voices non-existent.
I speak of them,
I speak from them.

the ones like us who escaped the prison
will do everything they can now
to burn it down
once and for all.

each time you fight for your share
and raise your voice to be heard
and they silence you with
'having it harder on the other end',
ask them if they'd walk a mile in your shoe.

the *hesitation* will be your answer.

the bear or the man

the debate ended in his mind when he held
his newborn daughter for the first time.

in a house filled with laughter
I find a corner of loneliness
the weight of their needs on me
I wonder who will notice
the cracks in my smile
when I laugh at jokes that sting,
the ones that silently say
'know your place'.

I look around at
other women in the room
all rooted in the same soil
I'm the only one awake
who sees the chains and
the roots anchoring deeper and
uprooting their sense of self.

I turn to my pen and paper,
the ink has always awakened masses.

She Awakens

Her

they left
but she stayed with herself.

there's beauty in living softly
in slowing down
in letting the world pass you by
while you move with the rhythm of nature
and walk your own way home.

she fell
and there,
she grew

once you truly get lost in yourself,
you never wish to be found again.

change isn't always bad

it just means
you're being redirected
towards your calling.

all your attempts
to control your life
have failed.

for once
let the universe
lead the way.

Her

you are not your past.

you are the strength you find
in leaving it behind.

take the pressure off

to live a certain way
be a certain way
and do things a certain way

have more fun.
no one will remember
whether you wore
the right clothes
or said the right words

but you will remember
on the last day
just how freely you could've lived
if you had *just* taken the pressure off.

Her

"change" is nothing but
finding a home in all the places
you once feared to visit.

there was a time
when women walked the earth
like goddesses in motion

the era only ended when
they stopped believing
they still can.

haven't we all run fast enough
to keep up with the world?
wrapped our mouths to breathe less poison
stuffed cotton balls in our ears
to dull the sound of cities that never sleep?

let's now sit on the grass, shall we?
breathe in the stillness
and call it a day.

she turned her sorrow into fertilizer
and planted saplings of her mistakes
now she strolls in a garden,
holding hands with wisdom.

he only visits
where the gardens have bloomed.

build your own ladder
to happiness, darling.

if you depend
on others
to give it to you,
you'll end up with
scraps they leave behind.

it's okay to outgrow the things
that once fit perfectly into your life…
including the parts of you
that you buried along the way.

Her

you take the
borrowed words
of those who haven't
walked a mile in your shoes,
cover yourself full
with their layers of doubt and criticism
then wonder why your body can't breathe.

healing is messy,
but so is growth
   and nature
     and relations
        and everything that truly matters.

Her

a woman who knows her worth
always arrives quietly

it's her presence that makes all the noise.

pour your love
into your own heart, darling
fill up the silences
between your breaths
and you will stumble into
your greatest romance ever.

Her

there's a place inside you
where peace lives like your forlorn lover
waiting patiently
for you to find your way back home.

some of the best things
that happen to you
are the ones you never planned for.

~ leave some space in life for miracles

Her

she knows heartache
like an old friend

she invites it home
for it brings seeds of
strength
wisdom
and power
that grow tall in her backyard

a reminder that she will always
rise each time she's buried.

one day, you'll
look back and realize
you're exactly
where you prayed to be.

Her

root your feet so firmly
in the ground
that you rise high with ease
and if you ever fall,
it'll be like coming home.

she is truth to one
and a bundle of lies to another.
a whisper of hope to one
a shadow of doubt to another.
she's stubborn to one,
yet fluid to another.

who is she?

a symphony of contrasts
a life in motion
a seeker who's searching
for everything and nothing at once.

pain
pleasure
anger
sadness
betrayal
heartache
peace
joy
love

eventually,
everything will lead you back to yourself.

About the Author

Mitali Meelan lives in Mumbai with her husband, a day-time job, and a folder of novels and poetry books she's always working on. This is her first poetry collection in a series to follow. Follow her journey on socials to stay up-to-date about her writing and publishing journey, with glimpses into her personal life.

Say hi to her on Instagram or Facebook @mitalimeelan

Follow her viral poetry page on Instagram @mm.pens

Other Books by the Author

Message in a Bookstore (A Novel, Kindle Exclusive)

The Guest (A Novel, Black Ink Books Publication)

A Long Way Home (A Novel, HarperCollins Publication)

Love and Lies (A Short Fiction Co-authored with Ravinder Singh, HarperCollins Publication)

And Then We Met Again (Original Audiobook by Storytel)